MW00786153

THE LOS ANGELES KINGS

BY

MARK STEWART

CONTENT CONSULTANT
DENIS GIBBONS
SOCIETY FOR INTERNATIONAL HOCKEY RESEARCH

NORWOODHOUSE PRESS

CHICAGO, ILLINOIS

Norwood House Press
P.O. Box 316598
Chicago, Illinois 60631

For information regarding Norwood House Press, please visit our website at:
www.norwoodhousepress.com or call 866-565-2900.

All photos courtesy of Associated Press except the following:
Topps, Inc. (6, 15, 21, 36, 37, 38, 42 top, 43 top, 45),
The Sporting News (7), Hockey Hall of Fame (8, 10, 27, 28, 39), Esso/Imperial Oil Ltd. (9),
Beckett Publications (22, 35 top left & bottom, 42 bottom), Quarton Group/NHL (29),
Black Book Partners (31, 34, 43), Author's Collection (33), O-Pee-Chee Ltd. (40).
Cover Photo: AP Photo/Ross D. Franklin

The memorabilia and artifacts pictured in this book are presented for educational and informational purposes,
and come from the collection of the author.

Editor: Mike Kennedy
Designer: Ron Jaffe
Project Management: Black Book Partners, LLC.
Special thanks to Topps, Inc.

Library of Congress Cataloging-in-Publication Data

Stewart, Mark, 1960 July 7-
   The Los Angeles Kings / by Mark Stewart.
      p. cm. -- (Team spirit)
   Includes bibliographical references and index.
   Summary: "A revised Team Spirit Hockey edition featuring the Los Angeles
Kings that chronicles the history and accomplishments of the team. Includes
access to the Team Spirit website which provides additional information and
photos"-- Provided by publisher.
   ISBN 978-1-59953-621-7 (library edition : alk. paper) -- ISBN
978-1-60357-629-1 (ebook) 1. Los Angeles Kings (Hockey
team)--History--Juvenile literature. I. Title.
   GV848.L67S78 2014
   796.962'640979494--dc23
                                                      2013031500

Manufactured in the United States of America in Stevens Point, Wisconsin.
239N—012014

COVER PHOTO: The Kings celebrate a goal during their amazing run to the
Stanley Cup in 2012.

TABLE OF CONTENTS

ABOUT OUR GLOSSARY

In this book, there may be several words that you are reading for the first time. Some are sports words, some are new vocabulary words, and some are familiar words that are used in an unusual way. All of these words are defined on page 46. Throughout the book, sports words appear in **bold type**. Regular vocabulary words appear in ***bold italic type***.

MEET THE KINGS

Springtime in Southern California is a good time to soak up some sunshine. The weather is ideal for outdoor sports such as golf, tennis, surfing, and cycling. Thanks to the Los Angeles Kings, this time of the year has also become the height of hockey season.

In many cities around the country, hockey players are major celebrities. They are often hounded for autographs when they go out. In L.A., the Kings compete for attention with superstars from the worlds of movies, music, and television. Players might go days and weeks without being recognized. But the Kings don't mind that. They prefer to focus on their jobs on the ice.

This book tells the story of the Kings. Each spring, when the weather warms up, it's time to dig down deep and make another run for the **Stanley Cup**. In a city where people are measured by star power and overnight success, the Kings are at their best working one goal at a time.

Anze Kopitar, Jeff Carter, and Drew Doughty congratulate one another after a goal by the Kings.

5

GLORY DAYS

ce hockey in Hollywood? During the 1960s, it seemed like a crazy idea. To Jack Kent Cooke, it made perfect sense. He had just bought basketball's Los Angeles Lakers and wanted to own a second **professional** sports team. Cooke got good news when the

TERRY SAWCHUK LOS ANGELES GOAL

National Hockey League (NHL) decided to expand from six to 12 teams. Los Angeles was awarded a club, and Cooke named it the Kings. They played their first season in 1967–68. The team's first coach was Red Kelly, one of the NHL's most respected stars in the 1950s and early 1960s.

The Kings built their team by picking unwanted players from the original six NHL clubs. Their first pick was 38-year-old goalie Terry Sawchuk. Bill Flett and Eddie Joyal led the offense, while the defense was anchored by Bill White and Dale Rolfe. Over the next few years, the Kings added Ross Lonsberry, Eddie Shack, Butch Goring, Juha Widing, Bob Berry, and Bob Pulford.

By the mid-1970s, the Kings had become a very competitive team. Pulford was now L.A.'s coach. His star players were goalie Rogie Vachon and center Marcel Dionne. Vachon had been the back-up goalie for the Montreal Canadiens. Dionne had been one of the Detroit Red Wings' best young players. With Dionne finishing among the league's scoring leaders every season, the Kings made the **playoffs** nine years in a row.

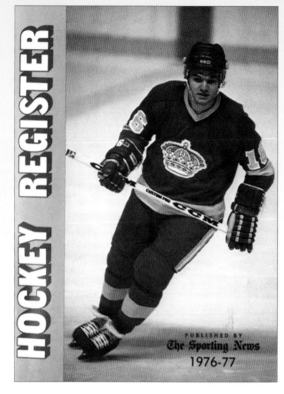

In 1978–79, the Kings hired Berry as their coach. He put Dionne on a **line** with Charlie Simmer and Dave Taylor. The trio became known as the "Triple Crown Line." In 1980–81, all three scored 100 points (goals plus **assists**). No line in NHL history had ever done that. During their six seasons together, they averaged better than 280 points a year.

Dionne played for the Kings until 1987, when he was traded away. By then, a new group of stars had stepped into leadership roles. Left wing Luc Robitaille was good for 40 to 50 goals a year. Bernie Nicholls was one of the top all-around centers in the NHL. Steve Duchesne

LEFT: Terry Sawchuk gave the Kings an experienced goalie in their first season.
ABOVE: Marcel Dionne was the center on the Triple Crown Line.

was a high-scoring defenseman. Another center, Jimmy Carson, scored more than 90 goals before the age of 20. Despite all of this talent, the Kings still lacked a leader who could make them a true championship contender.

That changed during the summer of 1988. The Kings traded for Wayne Gretzky of the Edmonton Oilers. In his first year in Los Angeles, "The Great One" scored 54 goals and had 114 assists for 168 points. He won the Hart Trophy as the NHL's **Most Valuable**

Player (MVP). Four years later, the Kings made it all the way to the Stanley Cup Finals. They began the season without Gretzky, who was recovering from a neck injury. By the time he rejoined the club, the Kings had come together under new coach Barry Melrose. Robitaille led a group of goal-scorers that included Jari Kurri, Tony Granato, Tomas Sandstrom, Mike Donnelly, and Rob Blake.

Gretzky was back at full speed by playoff time. He had 15 goals and 25 assists in the **postseason** to set team records. The Kings defeated the Calgary Flames, Vancouver Canucks, and Toronto

LEFT: Wayne Gretzky led the Kings to the playoffs five seasons in a row.
ABOVE: Luc Robitaille scored more than 500 goals in his career for the Kings.

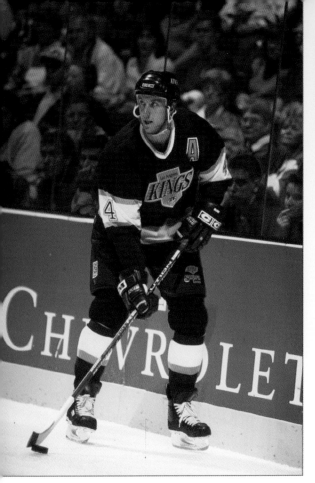

Maple Leafs in three tough series. The Los Angeles players were on the edge of exhaustion by the time they met the Montreal Canadiens in the finals. The Kings won the opening game but lost the next three in **overtime**. Montreal took Game 5 to win the Stanley Cup.

Although the Kings fell short of a championship, they proved with *sellout* after sellout that the NHL could succeed in a warm-weather city. In the years that followed, the league moved teams into Texas, Arizona, and Florida. Unfortunately for fans in Los Angeles, the Kings found it difficult to repeat their success. They won their **division** in 1990–91, but Gretzky was traded in 1996, leaving Blake to lead a new group of players that included Ziggy Palffy, Glen Murray and Jozef Stumpel. After Blake was traded in 2001, the Kings fell on hard times.

This dark cloud had a silver-and-black lining. The Kings used high picks in the NHL **draft** to rebuild the club. Defenseman Drew Doughty, right wing Dustin Brown, and center Anze Kopitar were all top draft choices. The Kings also grabbed goalie Jonathan Quick

and added Justin Williams, Jeff Carter, Jack Johnson, and Mike Richards through trades.

In 2011–12, the Kings returned to the Stanley Cup Finals. They played the New Jersey Devils, a club known for its tight defense. L.A. outlasted the Devils in two overtime battles, and then won Game 3. New Jersey battled back before the Kings finished off the series. Quick won the Conn Smythe Trophy as MVP of the playoffs.

Jack Kent Cooke (who sold the team in 1979 and passed away in 1997) would have been proud to see his Kings ride down the streets of Los Angeles in double-decker buses for the Stanley Cup victory parade. Thousands of fans wearing team jerseys cheered the players as confetti showered down from the surrounding office buildings.

LEFT: Rob Blake was named team captain after Wayne Gretzky was traded in 1996.   **ABOVE**: Dustin Brown roars with joy after L.A.'s Stanley Cup victory.

HOME ICE

The Kings played for more than 30 years in a building called the Great Western Forum. It opened during their first season. The Forum was designed to look like an arena in ancient Rome. The Kings shared it with the Lakers, the basketball team that was also owned by Jack Kent Cooke.

The Kings moved into their current home for the 1999–2000 season. Three professional basketball teams—the Lakers, the Los Angeles Clippers, and the Los Angeles Sparks—also play their home games in the arena. When the Kings won the 2012 Stanley Cup, it marked the first time since 2007 that an NHL team took the title on its home ice.

BY THE NUMBERS

- The Kings' arena has 18,118 seats for hockey.
- The arena cost $375 million to build in the late 1990s.
- Games and events at the arena attract nearly 4 million spectators a year.

Willie Mitchell and Jonathan Quick congratulate each other after a victory on the Kings' home ice during the 2012 playoffs.

DRESSED FOR SUCCESS

The Kings' original colors were purple and gold. They are considered "royal" colors. The team's *logo* was a king's crown. During their first 20 seasons, the Kings made a number of small changes to their jersey design, but the basic look remained the same. In 1988–89, the team swapped purple and gold for black and silver—the same colors as the Los Angeles Raiders football team.

EDDIE SHACK   **R. WING**
L.A. KINGS

The Kings worked purple back into their uniform starting in 1998–99. Over the next *decade*, they made a number of small changes in color and design. When fans began asking for the "old" silver-and-black colors, the team made the switch. The Kings also went with a logo that added the letters *LA* to the familiar crown.

LEFT: Justin Williams wears the team's 2012–13 away uniform.
RIGHT: This trading card of Eddie Shack shows L.A.'s original colors.

WE WON!

The NHL playoffs are sometimes called a "second season" because every team gets a fresh start. But that does not mean all playoff teams are equal. At the start of the 2012 postseason, no one gave the Kings a chance to win the Stanley Cup.

Los Angeles was the last team to make the playoffs, grabbing the eighth spot in the Western **Conference** with a victory in its second-to-last game of the regular season. The Kings were young and unproven. Only one player, Anze Kopitar, ranked among the league's Top 50 scorers. Darryl Sutter was the team's third coach since the start of the season!

Every expert predicted the Kings would fall in their opening-round series against the Vancouver Canucks, who finished the season with 111 points—the most in the NHL. But Jonathan Quick got hot for L.A., allowing just four goals in the first three games. The Kings went on to win the series in five games with a 2–1 overtime victory. Jarret Stoll got the series-winning goal.

Drew Doughty hugs Jarret Stoll after his overtime goal in Game 5 against the Vancouver Canucks.

Next came the St. Louis Blues. Quick was spectacular again. He held the Blues to just six goals in four games. L.A. swept the series to advance to the conference finals against the Phoenix Coyotes.

Against Phoenix, the Kings got some key contributions on offense. Jeff Carter notched a **hat trick** in Game 2 in a 4–0 victory. Dustin Penner sent the Kings to the Stanley Cup Finals with an overtime goal in Game 5. Now they had a chance to make history against the New Jersey Devils.

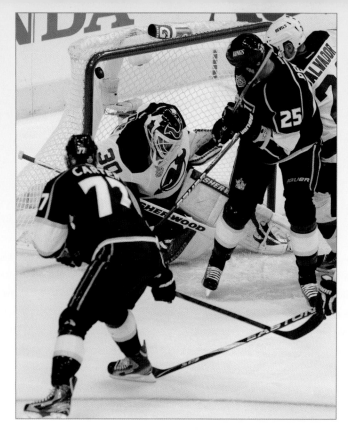

LEFT: Jeff Carter flicks the puck over goalie Martin Brodeur in Game 3, as Dustin Penner clears the front of the net.
RIGHT: Jonathan Quick shows the Conn Smythe Trophy to the fans in L.A.

Quick outplayed Devils goalie Martin Brodeur in the first two games in New Jersey. The Kings took Game 1 in overtime by a score of 2–1. Kopitar netted the winner. It was a similar story in Game 2. This time, Carter scored in overtime for another 2-1 victory. Quick was magnificent in Game 3. He turned away 22 shots and made some incredible saves in a 4–0 shutout.

Before Game 4 in Los Angeles, Sutter fired up his team in the locker room. "You get nothing for three," he said. "That's why the fourth is the toughest one."

Sutter was right. New Jersey fought back to win the next two games. The Kings regrouped and poured it on in Game 6 with a 6–1 blowout. Carter scored the goal that put Los Angeles ahead for good. The Kings were the first team to win the Stanley Cup as the eighth **seed** in their conference.

GO-TO GUYS

To be a true star in the NHL, you need more than a great slapshot. You have to be a "go-to guy"—someone teammates trust to make the winning play when the seconds are ticking away in a big game. Kings fans have had a lot to cheer about over the years, including these great stars.

THE PIONEERS

BUTCH GORING   Center

• BORN 10/22/1949   • PLAYED FOR TEAM: 1969–70 TO 1979–80

Butch Goring was a quick, clever, and hardworking center. When he joined the Kings, he was a better defender than a scorer. But Goring kept improving his offense. He scored 20 or more goals for the Kings nine seasons in a row.

ROGIE VACHON   Goalie

• BORN 9/8/1945   • PLAYED FOR TEAM: 1971–72 TO 1977–78

L.A.'s defense had a lot of holes in the 1970s. Fortunately, the Kings had Rogie Vachon in goal. His lightning reflexes and ability to snatch pucks out of the air made him hard to beat, especially when he was one-on-one with an opponent.

MARCEL DIONNE   Center

- BORN 8/3/1951   • PLAYED FOR TEAM: 1975–76 TO 1986–87

Marcel Dionne was the Kings' first great scorer. He reached 100 points seven times and had three 130-point seasons in a row. Dionne won the Art Ross Trophy as the NHL's top scorer in 1979–80.

CHARLIE SIMMER   Center/Wing

- BORN 3/20/1954   • PLAYED FOR TEAM: 1977–78 TO 1984–85

It took a couple of years for Charlie Simmer to earn a regular spot with the Kings. Once he did, he scored goals at a record-breaking pace. Simmer battled through injuries to net 56 goals two years in a row. He was a **First-Team All-Star** in 1979–80 and 1980–81.

DAVE TAYLOR   Right Wing

- BORN 12/4/1955
- PLAYED FOR TEAM: 1977–78 TO 1993–94

Dave Taylor played 1,111 games for the Kings and finished his career with 1,069 points. He was picked by L.A. in the 15th round of the 1975 draft, which made him one of the greatest "bargains" in NHL history. The Kings retired his number 18 in 1995.

DAVE TAYLOR
RIGHT WING

ABOVE: Dave Taylor

LUC ROBITAILLE   Left Wing

- Born 2/17/1966
- Played for Team: 1986–87 to 1993–94, 1997–98 to 2000–01
                          & 2003–04 to 2005–06

Luc Robitaille was a superstar from the first day he put on a Kings uniform. He scored 45 goals as a **rookie** and won the Calder Trophy. When he retired, he had more goals and points than any left wing in history. Robitaille helped run the Kings after he retired, including when they won the Stanley Cup in 2012.

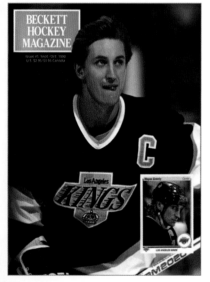

WAYNE GRETZKY   Center

- Born 1/26/1961
- Played for Team: 1988–89 to 1995–96

Wayne Gretzky was under great pressure to turn the Kings into a winner when he joined the team. The Great One was up to the challenge. He won the Hart Trophy in his first year and was the NHL scoring champion three times during his years in Los Angeles.

ROB BLAKE   Defenseman

- Born 12/10/1969
- Played for Team: 1989–90 to 2000–01 & 2006–07 to 2007–08

Rob Blake was a big defenseman with a great scoring touch. His hard shot, smart passing, and punishing **checks** helped the Kings reach the Stanley Cup Finals in 1993. In 1997–98, Blake won the Norris Trophy as the NHL's top **blue-liner**.

ANZE KOPITAR   Center

- BORN 8/24/1987
- FIRST SEASON WITH TEAM: 2006–07

Anze Kopitar joined the Kings at the age of 19 and quickly became their most exciting scorer and playmaker. In the years that followed, he became a good defender, too. Kopitar was the first player from Slovenia to win a Stanley Cup.

DUSTIN BROWN   Left Wing/Right Wing

- BORN 11/4/1984   • FIRST SEASON WITH TEAM: 2003–04

Dustin Brown became a team leader with his teeth-rattling checks and unselfish play. At times, he played more like a defenseman, but he was also a **clutch** scorer. Brown was just the second American-born team captain to win a Stanley Cup.

JONATHAN QUICK   Goalie

- BORN 1/21/1986   • FIRST SEASON WITH TEAM: 2007–08

A championship team needs a goalie who can raise his game in the playoffs. Jonathan Quick did just that in leading the Kings to the Stanley Cup in 2012—and was rewarded with the Conn Smythe Trophy. He also set an NHL record by winning 12 road playoff games in a row.

LEFT: Wayne Gretzky was chosen by *Beckett Hockey Magazine* to be on its first-ever cover.   **ABOVE**: Anze Kopitar and Dustin Brown

Some people say that Los Angeles is not a "hockey town." Try telling that to the 20-plus coaches who have led the team into battle. When the Kings are winning, their coaches are cheered as geniuses. When they are not, being the coach of the Kings is one of the true high-pressure jobs in the NHL.

Two coaches *distinguished* themselves during the teams first 30 years: Bob Pulford and Barry Melrose. When Pulford took over the Kings in 1972–73, he knew the team needed to improve on defense. He had seen this weakness firsthand as a player for L.A. in the two previous seasons. By 1974–75, the Kings had developed into one of the best defensive teams in the league. Pulford was given the Jack Adams Award that season as the NHL's top coach.

Melrose had never coached an NHL club when he arrived in L.A. in 1992–93. However, he was still known as one of the smartest people in the game. Melrose made believers out of Kings fans when he led the team to the Stanley Cup Finals in his first season.

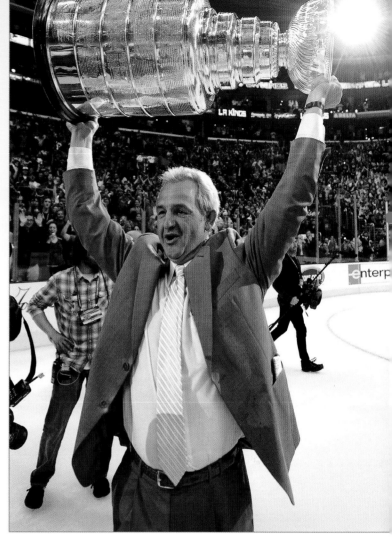

Darryl Sutter gets his turn to raise the Stanley Cup in 2012.

The coach who finally took L.A. all the way to the championship was Darryl Sutter. He coached the Chicago Blackhawks, San Jose Sharks, and Calgary Flames before joining the Kings. He was hired to replace Terry Murray in December of 2011.

Sutter guided the Kings to a 25–13–11 record the rest of the way. That was just good enough to earn a playoff spot. From there, the Kings rolled through the postseason and beat the New Jersey Devils for the Stanley Cup. Under Sutter, L.A. won 10 postseason games on the road to set an NHL record.

APRIL 10, 1982

Before Wayne Gretzky joined the Kings in 1988, he was one of their most dreaded opponents. In the first round of the 1982 playoffs, L.A. faced Gretzky and the Edmonton Oilers. The Great One had broken the league record for goals during the regular season, and his Oilers were expected by many to win the Stanley Cup. The series was tied 1–1 when the teams met in The Forum for Game 3.

The Oilers scored two goals in the first period and three more in the second. Gretzky netted two of the goals and assisted on two others. Edmonton was in complete control when the third period started. Or, at least, that's what it looked like. Less than three minutes into the final period, Jay Wells fired a shot that beat Grant Fuhr for the Kings' first goal. A few minutes later, Doug Smith scored on a **power play** to cut the Oilers lead to 5–2.

With six minutes to play, Charlie Simmer stuffed the puck past Fuhr. Now it was 5–3. Moments later, Mark Hardy caught Gretzky

Mark Hardy scored the fourth goal in L.A.'s great comeback and assisted on the one that tied the game.

out of position and beat Fuhr with a quick wrist shot to cut the deficit to a single goal.

The crowd at the Forum gasped when the Oilers had a breakaway, but Mario Lessard stopped the shot. With a minute left, the Kings replaced Lessard with an extra skater. Hardy took a shot that Fuhr stopped, but rookie Steve Bozek swooped in to score on the rebound and send the game into overtime.

Both teams had great chances in the extra period, but the Kings scored the winning goal on a slapshot by Daryl Evans. It marked the greatest comeback in the history of the Stanley Cup playoffs. The Kings went on to win the series. Since The Forum was located on Manchester Boulevard, fans would come to call this game "The Miracle on Manchester."

LEGEND HAS IT

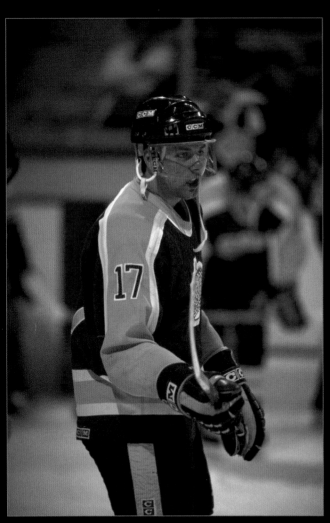

WHO WAS THE NHL'S TOP TEENAGER?

LEGEND HAS IT that Jimmy Carson was. Carson joined the Kings for the 1986–87 season at the age of 18 and scored 37 goals. In 1987–88, he had an even better season with 55 goals. Carson's 92 goals as a teenager set a league record. When the Kings traded for Wayne Gretzky, Carson was the only active player that the Edmonton Oilers demanded in return.

ABOVE: No teenager in NHL history scored as often as Jimmy Carson did with the Kings. RIGHT: Marcel Dionne didn't stay an "unknown superstar" for long in Los Angeles.

WAS MARCEL DIONNE HOCKEY'S FIRST FREE AGENT?

LEGEND HAS IT that he was. A free agent is a player who is free to play with any team that wants him. Before 1975, the NHL did not allow free agents. That June, Dionne left the Detroit Red Wings and became the first big-name star to test the league's brand-new free agency rule. He chose to sign with the Kings. In return, L.A. had to give up Dan Maloney, Terry Harper, and a draft pick to Detroit.

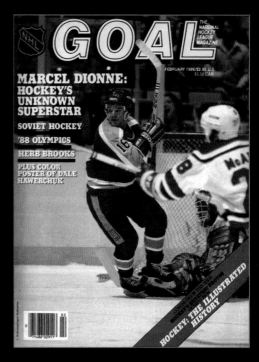

WERE THE 2012 KINGS THE BEST "LAST-PLACE" TEAM IN HISTORY?

LEGEND HAS IT that they were. The Kings grabbed the eighth and last playoff spot in the Western Conference with one game left in the regular season. No eighth-ranked club had ever won the Stanley Cup. The Kings not only captured the championship, they beat the first-, second-, and third-place teams in the conference to make it to the finals!

Near the end of the 1978–79 season, the Kings were hit by a series of injuries. Coach Bob Berry called up Charlie Simmer from the **minor leagues**. Simmer was a slow skater for a center, so Berry moved him to left wing to play with Marcel Dionne and Dave Taylor. No one knew it then, but this was the start of the fabled Triple Crown Line.

Simmer's quick reflexes made him a dangerous player around the net. When a puck was loose on the ice, he usually got his stick on it first. He scored in each of the last five games of the season.

When the 1979–80 season began, Simmer picked up right where he left off and scored in each of the first six games. That sent sportswriters scrambling for the record book. They discovered that the longest goal-scoring streak in modern NHL history was 10 games. Superstars Andy Bathgate and Mike Bossy shared the record. Simmer now had a streak of 11, which made him the new record-holder. Or did it? The league refused to recognize Simmer's 11-game streak because it took place over two seasons.

Charlie Simmer was one of the streakiest goal-scorers in NHL history.

No problem. Simmer started a new streak that year in late November. He scored in every game for more than a month—13 in all—to become the new record-holder. Simmer later admitted that he got one or two good breaks along the way.

"I had some luck," he said. "For example, in a game against Buffalo, after shooting and missing and getting knocked down, I looked up and there was the puck—sitting on the ice in front of me! I reached out and slammed it into the net. I think maybe that goal felt the best of them all."

TEAM SPIRIT

Before the Kings played their first game in 1967, the westernmost NHL team was located in Chicago, Illinois—more than 2,000 miles away. Many questioned whether the Kings could survive. In their first few seasons, the Kings filled roughly half their arena for home games. Attendance climbed steadily in the 1970s and 1980s. The trade for Wayne Gretzky changed everything. The Kings started playing to sellout crowds on a regular basis.

Today, there are a lot of movie, television, and music stars in the stands for the team's home games. Taylor Swift, Ellen Page, Jim Carrey, Steve Carrell, and Sandra Bullock are among the famous faces that have been spotted in the crowd. Also, Kings fans are among the most "wired" in hockey—they use *social media* to communicate all year long.

LEFT: Kings fans never doubted that pro hockey would succeed in California.
RIGHT: Members of the team's booster club wore this pin in the 1980s.

TIMELINE

The hockey season is played from October through June. That means each season takes place at the end of one year and the beginning of the next. In this timeline, the accomplishments of the Kings are shown by season.

1974–75
The team has its first winning season.

1980–81
The Kings host the **All-Star Game**.

1967–68
The Kings play their first season.

1976–77
Rogie Vachon sets a team record with eight **shutouts**.

1982–83
Marcel Dionne has his fifth 50-goal season in a row.

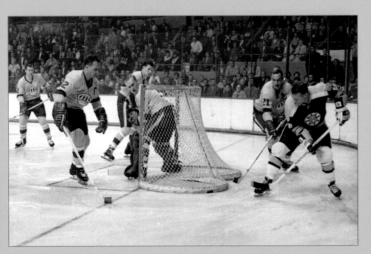

The Kings battle the Boston Bruins in their first season.

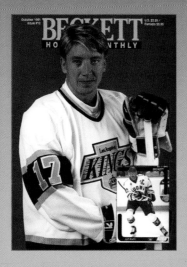

Jari Kurri was a leader for the 1992–93 Kings.

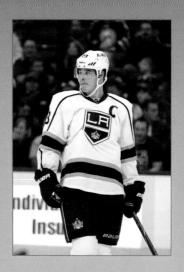

Dustin Brown

1986–87
Luc Robitaille scores 45 goals as a rookie.

1992–93
The Kings reach the Stanley Cup Finals for the first time.

2012–13
Dustin Brown plays his 600th career game.

1988–89
Bernie Nicholls sets a team record with 70 goals.

1993–94
Wayne Gretzky breaks the NHL record for most goals in a career.

2011–12
Darryl Sutter leads the Kings to the Stanley Cup.

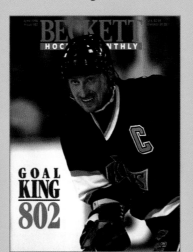

This magazine celebrated Wayne Gretzky's record-breaking goal.

**BOB
BERRY**

LEFT WING

BERRY GOOD

Bob Berry was known for his ability to slap rebounds into the net and redirect shots past helpless goalies. Berry was nicknamed after the place he did most of his scoring from—"**Crease.**"

SECOND THOUGHTS

When the Kings traded for Randy Holt during the 1978–79 season, they hoped the *burly* defenseman would make opponents think twice before trying to push them around. *Los Angeles* started thinking twice after Holt racked up 67 penalty minutes—in a single game!

TAKES TWO TO TANGO

In the first game of the 1982 playoffs, the Kings beat the Edmonton Oilers in a wild contest, 10–8. The 18 goals were the most ever scored by two teams in a postseason game.

UNBEATABLE

Rogie Vachon was at his best when facing a shooter one-on-one. He did not allow a single goal on a **penalty shot** in his NHL career.

DOUBLE DUTY

As of 2013, 14 players who suited up for the Kings went on to make it into the **Hall of Fame**. Two of them—Bob Pulford and Larry Robinson—also coached the team.

LUCKY SEVEN

Darryl Sutter was one of seven hockey-playing brothers. Six played in the NHL, and they won the Stanley Cup six times between them. When Darryl led the Kings to the championship in 2012, he became the first Sutter sibling to raise the Stanley Cup as a coach.

FORCE OF ONE

When Bernie Nicholls got on a roll, he was hard to stop. He once scored a hat trick in three straight games. In 1988–89, Nicholls scored a team-record 70 goals and had eight points in one game.

LEFT: Bob Berry
ABOVE: Rogie Vachon

TALKING HOCKEY

"You can't say enough about this group and how hard they worked."

▶ *JONATHAN QUICK, on the dedication of his teammates during the 2012 playoffs*

LARRY ROBINSON • D

"That's the good thing about hockey. There's always tomorrow."

▶ *LARRY ROBINSON, on putting tough losses behind you*

"You dream of winning the Cup, and you know what, I'm glad I was the first King to ever lift it."

▶ *DUSTIN BROWN, on helping the club win its first NHL title*

"This is not tennis, where you're alone on the court. Hockey is a team game."

▶ *LUC ROBITAILLE, on working together with your teammates*

"To think of the talented guys we've had here—Wayne Gretzky, Luc Robitaille, guys that are unbelievable goal scorers—to still have a record here it's pretty special."

▶ **BERNIE NICHOLLS,** *on his team record of 70 goals in a season*

"You always want to stay a step ahead, and you have to know your competition every night and your competition coming up."

▶ **ROB BLAKE,** *on the importance of studying game film*

"We had twenty-five guys believing in one thing. I can't be more proud of the guys."

▶ **ANZE KOPITAR,** *on the teamwork it took to win the Stanley Cup*

"To be remembered as an L.A. King is something special."

▶ **WAYNE GRETZKY,** *on having his number retired by the team*

LEFT: Larry Robinson
ABOVE: Bernie Nicholls

GREAT DEBATES

People who root for the Kings love to compare their favorite moments, teams, and players. Some debates have been going on for years! How would you settle these classic hockey arguments?

MARCEL DIONNE WAS THE TEAM'S MOST VALUABLE PLAYER ...

... because he had the ability to make things happen every time he stepped on the ice. L.A. fans had never seen a player like Dionne. Before he arrived, the Kings were happy to keep the score close. After he came to the Kings, the team believed it could win any game. Dionne had "star quality" that scared opponents and gave his teammates confidence.

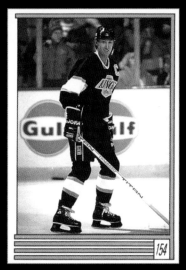

WHAT ABOUT THE GREAT ONE? WAYNE GRETZKY WAS THE ALL-TIME MVP ...

... because he took a good NHL club and turned it into a Stanley Cup contender. Gretzky's greatest talent was making his teammates better. Playing with Gretzky ( ), young stars such as Luc Robitaille, Rob Blake, and Tony Granato were able to raise their games to new heights. And don't forget that Gretzky led the NHL in scoring in three of his five seasons in L.A.

ROGIE VACHON WAS THE KINGS' GREATEST GOALIE ...

... because he transformed the team into a defensive force. Vachon came to L.A. from a championship team—the Montreal Canadiens—so he gave the Kings instant respect from their opponents. Because of his ability to make great saves, the defensemen could play more aggressively and take chances. Almost overnight, L.A. went from having one of the NHL's worst defenses to having one of the best.

NO L.A. GOALIE WAS EVER BETTER THAN JONATHAN QUICK ...

... because he raised his game as the stakes got higher and higher. Quick (RIGHT) was a good goalie during the regular season. But once the playoffs started, he turned into a great one. The farthest the Kings ever got with Vachon in goal was the second round of the playoffs. With Quick, they won the Stanley Cup.

T he great Kings teams and players have left their marks on the record books. These are the "best of the best" ...

Marcel Dionne

Luc Robitaille

KINGS AWARD WINNERS

ART ROSS TROPHY
TOP SCORER

Marcel Dionne	1979–80
Wayne Gretzky	1989–90
Wayne Gretzky	1990–91
Wayne Gretzky	1993–94

HART MEMORIAL TROPHY
MOST VALUABLE PLAYER

Wayne Gretzky	1988–89

CONN SMYTHE TROPHY
MVP DURING PLAYOFFS

Jonathan Quick	2011–12

CALDER TROPHY
TOP ROOKIE

Luc Robitaille	1986–87

JACK ADAMS AWARD
COACH OF THE YEAR

Bob Pulford	1974–75

LESTER B. PEARSON AWARD
MOST OUTSTANDING PLAYER

Marcel Dionne	1978–79
Marcel Dionne	1979–80

JAMES NORRIS MEMORIAL TROPHY
TOP DEFENSEMAN

Rob Blake	1997–98

KINGS ACHIEVEMENTS

ACHIEVEMENT	YEAR
Smythe Division Champions	1990–91
Campbell Conference Champions	1992–93
Western Conference Champions	2011–12
Stanley Cup Champions	2011–12

BOB
PULFORD
CENTER

RIGHT: Bob Pulford came to the Kings as a player and ended up as an award-winning coach.

BELOW: Rogie Vachon covers the puck. He was the first true star for the Kings.

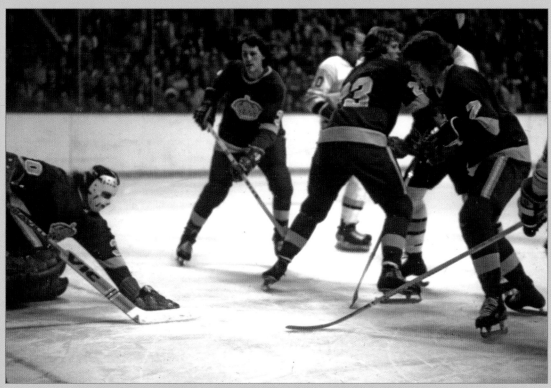

PINPOINTS

The history of a hockey team is made up of many smaller stories. These stories take place all over the map—not just in the city a team calls "home." Match the pushpins on these maps to the **TEAM FACTS**, and you will begin to see the story of the Kings unfold!

1 Los Angeles, California—*The Kings have played here since 1967.*

2 Milford, Connecticut—*Jonathan Quick was born here.*

3 Ithaca, New York—*Dustin Brown was born here.*

4 Downers Grove, Illinois—*Tony Granato was born here.*

5 St. Boniface, Manitoba—*Butch Goring was born here.*

6 Montreal, Quebec—*Bob Berry was born here.*

7 Vermillion, Alberta—*Bill Flett was born here.*

8 London, Ontario—*Jeff Carter was born here.*

9 Levack, Ontario—*Dave Taylor was born here.*

10 Jakobstad, Finland—*Tomas Sandstrom was born here.*

11 Samedan, Switzerland—*Mark Hardy was born here.*

12 Skalica, Slovakia—*Ziggy Palffy was born here.*

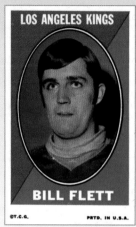

Bill Flett

GLOSSARY

ALL-STAR GAME—The annual game that features the best players from the NHL.

ASSISTS—Passes that lead to a goal.

BLUE-LINER—Another term for a defenseman.

BURLY—Large and strong; heavily built.

CHECKS—Body blows that stop an opponent from advancing with the puck.

CLUTCH—Performing well under pressure.

CONFERENCE—A large group of teams. There are two conferences in the NHL, and each season each conference sends a team to the Stanley Cup Finals.

CREASE—The area in front of the goal, between the two red circles in the defensive end.

DECADE—A period of 10 years; also specific periods, such as the 1950s.

DISTINGUISHED—Set apart.

DIVISION—A small group of teams in a conference. Each NHL conference has three divisions.

DRAFT—The annual meeting during which NHL teams pick the top high school, college, and international players.

FIRST-TEAM ALL-STAR—The annual award that recognizes the best NHL players at each position.

HALL OF FAME—The museum in Toronto, Canada, where hockey's best players are honored. A player voted into the Hall of Fame is sometimes called a "Hall of Famer."

HAT TRICK—Three goals in a game.

LINE—The trio made up by a left wing, center, and right wing.

LOGO—A symbol or design that represents a company or team.

MINOR LEAGUES—All the professional leagues that operate below the NHL.

MOST VALUABLE PLAYER (MVP)—The award given each year to the league's best player; also given to the best player in the playoffs and All-Star Game.

NATIONAL HOCKEY LEAGUE (NHL)—The professional league that has been operating since 1917.

OVERTIME—An extra period played when a game is tied after three periods. In the NHL playoffs, teams continue to play overtime periods until a goal is scored.

PENALTY SHOT—A shot awarded to a player when an obvious scoring opportunity is stopped by an illegal play.

PLAYOFFS—The games played after the season to determine the league champion.

POSTSEASON—Another term for playoffs.

POWER PLAY—A game situation in which one team has at least one extra skater on the ice. A power play occurs when a player commits a penalty and is sent to the penalty box.

PROFESSIONAL—A player or team that plays a sport for money.

ROOKIE—A player in his first season.

SEED—A spot awarded to a team in the NHL playoffs. Each conference has eight seeds.

SELLOUT—A game for which every ticket is sold.

SHUTOUTS—Games in which a team is prevented from scoring.

SOCIAL MEDIA—All the ways that people share information, including the Internet, Twitter, and blogs.

STANLEY CUP—The trophy presented to the NHL champion. The first Stanley Cup was awarded in 1893.

LINE CHANGE

TEAM SPIRIT introduces a great way to stay up to date with your team! Visit our **LINE CHANGE** link and get connected to the latest and greatest updates. **LINE CHANGE** serves as a young reader's ticket to an exclusive web page—with more stories, fun facts, team records, and photos of the Kings. Content is updated during and after each season. The **LINE CHANGE** feature also enables readers to send comments and letters to the author! Log onto:

www.norwoodhousepress.com/library.aspx

and click on the tab: **TEAM SPIRIT** to access **LINE CHANGE**.

Read all the books in the series to learn more about professional sports. For a complete listing of the baseball, basketball, football, and hockey teams in the **TEAM SPIRIT** series, visit our website at:

www.norwoodhousepress.com/library.aspx

ON THE ROAD

LOS ANGELES KINGS
1111 S. Figueroa Street, Suite 3100
Los Angeles, California 90015
213-742-7100
http://kings.nhl.com

HOCKEY HALL OF FAME
Brookfield Place
30 Yonge Street
Toronto, Ontario, Canada M5E 1X8
(416) 360-7765
http://www.hhof.com

ON THE BOOKSHELF

To learn more about the sport of hockey, look for these books at your library or bookstore:

- Cameron, Steve. *Hockey Hall of Fame Treasures.* Richmond Hill, Ontario, Canada: Firefly Books, 2011.

- MacDonald, James. *Hockey Skills: How to Play Like a Pro.* Berkeley Heights, New Jersey: Enslow Elementary, 2009.

- Keltie, Thomas. *Inside Hockey! The legends, facts, and feats that made the game.* Toronto, Ontario, Canada: Maple Tree Press, 2008.

INDEX

PAGE NUMBERS IN **BOLD** REFER TO ILLUSTRATIONS.

THE TEAM

MARK STEWART has written over 200 books for kids—and more than a dozen books on hockey, including a history of the Stanley Cup and an authorized biography of goalie Martin Brodeur. He grew up in New York City during the 1960s rooting for the Rangers, but has gotten to know a couple of New Jersey Devils, so he roots for a shootout when these teams play each other. Mark comes from a family of writers. His grandfather was Sunday Editor of *The New York Times*, and his mother was Articles Editor of *Ladies' Home Journal* and *McCall's*. Mark has profiled hundreds of athletes over the past 25 years. He has also written several books about his native New York and New Jersey, his home today. Mark is a graduate of Duke University, with a degree in history. He lives and works in a home overlooking Sandy Hook, New Jersey. You can contact Mark through the Norwood House Press website.

DENIS GIBBONS is a writer and editor with *The Hockey News* and a former newsletter editor of the Toronto-based Society for International Hockey Research (SIHR). He was a contributing writer to the publication *Kings of the Ice: A History of World Hockey* and has worked as chief hockey researcher at five Winter Olympics for the ABC, CBS, and NBC television networks. Denis also has worked as a researcher for the FOX Sports Network during the Stanley Cup playoffs. He resides in Burlington, Ontario, Canada with his wife Chris.